YOUR KNOWLEDGE HAS VALUE

Bibliographic information published by the German National Library:

The German National Library lists this publication in the National Bibliography; detailed bibliographic data are available on the Internet at http://dnb.dnb.de .

Imprint:

Copyright © 2019 GRIN Verlag
Print and binding: Books on Demand GmbH, Norderstedt Germany
ISBN: 9783346082619

Erhunse Confidence

Perceptions On Pre-Marital Sexual Relationships. Sexual Behaviour of Adolescents and Youths in in Anambra State, Nigeria

GRIN Verlag

GRIN - Your knowledge has value

Since its foundation in 1998, GRIN has specialized in publishing academic texts by students, college teachers and other academics as e-book and printed book. The website www.grin.com is an ideal platform for presenting term papers, final papers, scientific essays, dissertations and specialist books.

Visit us on the internet:

http://www.grin.com/

http://www.facebook.com/grincom

http://www.twitter.com/grin_com

PERCEPTION OF STUDENTS ON PRE-MARITAL SEXUAL RELATIONSHIP IN TERTIARY INSTITUTIONS IN ANAMBRA STATE

ERHUNSE CONFIDENCE

Abstract

Sexual behaviour of adolescents and youth are categorized as one of the main health priorities of a society because of high prevalence of Human Immunodeficiency Virus/Acquired Immunodeficiency Syndrome (HIV/AIDS), Sexually Transmitted Infections This paper focused on school counselling strategies for resolving disciplinary problems in Nigerian public secondary schools. Students' disciplinary problems are growing at alarming rate prompting the need for effective strategies for curbing them. When disciplinary problems are not curbed, they affect the teaching/learning process and the general time of the school. Disciplinary problems of students interfere with learning, divert administrative time, and contribute to teacher burn out. Schools often respond to disruptive students with exclusionary and punitive approaches that have limited value. Natures of Discipline Problems in Schools, Disciplinary Problems in Secondary Schools, etc were epistemological and empirical studied suggesting strategies which counselors should apply in resolving disciplinary problems in Nigerian secondary schools. Sexual relationship among students in tertiary institution in Anambra State, the challenges of sex before marriage comes with it own causes, consequences danger. It possible solutions, two theory was used hi this study, the gender Selema theory and theory of planned behavior to explain, sex before marriage. Base on the findings it was concluded that sex before marriage has researched among proportion and sex before marriage is now part of social life of students, Therefore it was recommended that early sex education and campaign should be given to children to create awareness on sex before marriage and should be carried out by the parents, government and general public to reduce the rate of premarital sex among students in tertiary institutions in Anambra State.

Table of Contents

Introduction

Sexual behaviour refers to the organization and expression of an individual's criticism and /or emotional attachment with reference to the sex and gender of the partner involved in sexual activity (Omoni & Onoyase, 2013).

The sexual behavior of an individual is to a large extent a function of the inherited sexual response pattern or the extent of the restraint exerted on the individual by society.

Today, due to the advances in technology and its impact on the quality of life, addressing the health and its influencing factors has become important. Also, providing health for health for the society is considered as one of the main issues in any country. Sexual behaviors of adolescents and youths are categorized as one of the main health priorities of society because of high prevalence of human immune deficiency syndrome (HIV/AIDS), sexually transmitted infections (STIs) and unwanted pregnancies.

Sexuality is not an instrument of enjoying lustful pleasure for human being, at least. In premarital sex, many a times, immature human beings explore the sexuality, just out of curiosity, and might be are unaware of the consequences. The feared consequences of risky sexual behaviors are: sexually transmitted diseases, unwanted pregnancy and sometimes psychological consequences of sexual violence (Umeononihu, 2012). This study was undertaken amongst students in a tertiary institution to ascertain the risky sexual behaviors amongst them so as to suggest solutions on how to remedy the problem.

Conceptual Framework

Pre-Marital Sex

Premarital sexuality is any sexual activity with an opposite sex partner or with a same sex partner before he/she has started a married life. The term is usually used to refer the intercourse before the legal age of a marriage. Adults who presumably marry eventually also fall under this definition. (Hazzaz,Bin, Zubairu, & S.A. (2005).

Premarital sex is referred to sexual relations between two people prior to marrying each other. During that period, it was the norm in western societies for men and women to marry by the age of 21 or 22, and there was no consideration that one who had sex would not marry. The term was used

4

instead of fornication, which has negative connotations, and was closely related to the concept and approval of virginity, which is sexual abstinence until marriage (Adinma and Okeke, 2005).

The meaning has since shifted to refer to any sexual relations a person has prior to marriage and removing the emphasis on the relationship of the people involved. The definition has a degree of ambiguity. It is not clear whether sex between individuals legally forbidden from marrying or the sexual relations of one uninterested in marrying would be considered premarital.

Alternative terms for premarital sex have been suggested, including non-marital sex (which overlaps with adultery), youthful sex, adolescent sex and young adult sex. These terms also suffer from a degree of ambiguity, as the definition of having sex differs from person to person. However, from my own view, pre-marital sex simply means engaging in sexual activity before the legal marriage or out of marriage.

Theoretical Framework

Gender Schema Theory

Gender schema theory was formally introduced by Sandra Ben in 1981 as a cognitive theory to explain how individuals become gendered in society, and how sex-linked characteristics are maintained and transmitted to other members of a culture. Gender associated information is predominantly transmuted through society by way of schemata, or networks of information that allow for some information to be more easily assimilated than other. Bem argues that there are individual differences in the degree to which people hold these gender schemata. These differences are manifested via the degree to which individual are sex- typed.

Gender schemas have an impact not only on how students process information but on the pre-marital and beliefs that direct "gender-appropriate" behavior. For example, a student who lives in a very traditional culture might believe that woman's role is in the caring and raise of children, while a man's role is in work and industry. Through these observations, student from schema related to what men and women can and cannot do. It also dictates a person's value and potential in that culture. For example, a girl raised in a traditional culture might believe that only path available to her as a woman is to get married and raise kids. By contrast, a girl raised in a more progressive culture might pursue a career, avoid having children, or decide not to get married.

5

Many of these influences are overt, while others are subtle. For instance, even the placement of gender titles in vocabulary ("how men and women are meant to behave") inherently places women in a secondary position by rule. All of these influences add up to how gender schema is formed.

Theory of Planned Behavior

The theory of planned behavior (TPB) was developed by social psychologists and has been widely employed as a tool to aid our understanding of a variety of behaviors including health behaviors (Ajzen 1991, Godin and Kok 1996) the TPB detail how the influences upon an individual determine that individual's decision to follow a particular behavior. Within the TPB, the determinants of behavior are intention to engage in that behavior and perceived behavioral control (PBC) over that behavior. Intentions represent a person's motivation. The construct is conceptualized as an individual's conscious plan or decision to exert effort in order to engage in a particularly behavior is within his or her control. Intentions are determined by three variables. The first is attitudes, which are an individual's overall evaluation of their behavior. The second is subjective norms. Which consists of a person's beliefs about whether significant others think he/ she should engage in the behavior is under their personal control and is labeled PBC.

The attitude, subjective norm and PBC components are determined by underlying beliefs. Attitude is a function of a person's salient behavioral beliefs; which represent perceived likely consequences of this behavior e.g., taking exercise will reduce my risk of heart disease. Subjective norm is a function of normative beliefs, which represent perceptions of specific salient others' preferences about whether one should or should not engage in a behavior (e.g., my family think I should take exercise). PBC is based on beliefs concerning access to the necessary resources and opportunity to perform the behavior successfully (e.g., I have easy access to a place where I can exercise).

So according to the TPB, individuals are likely to engage in a health behavior if they believe that the behavior will lead to particular outcomes which they value, if they believe that people whose views they value think they should carry out the behavior, and if they feel that they have the necessary resources and opportunities to perform the behavior.

Types of Sexual Relationship

Sexual relationships are divided into three, namely;

1.   **Premarital Sex**- premarital sex is what most youths engage n before marriage.

2.   **Marital Sex**- is referring to physical sexual activity that does not necessarily end up in an intercourse within marriage.

3.   **Extra Marital Sex**- extramarital affairs are relationship outside marriage where an illicit romantic/sexual relationship occurs.

Causes of Pre-Marital Sexual Relationship

➤   **Curiosity:** Many students in tertiary institutions have engaged themselves in premarital sex as result of curiosity. They thought they were searching for reality, but they ended up destroyed themselves. They are not satisfied with what their parents, pastors and Christian friends told them concerning sex, they want to experience it themselves.

➤   **Electronic media:** television, film, radio and video have contributed to the high rate of premarital sex. What youths watch on screen determine their behavior and character. Every product advertised on T.V. is just promoting sex. In fact, to advertise food items they use sex, film, television and radio promotes premarital sex. Most home videos are sex promoter.

➤   **Books and magazines:** some authors are in campuses destroyed the youths, they write some sexual stories, books and magazines, bring out many pictures that stimulate the youth to think about sex always. Having read all these books, youths, do become restless until they have put into practice what they learned in the books and magazines.

➤   **Environmental influence:** we live in a corrupt society where people do not see anything bad in ungodliness they do not see premarital sex as sin; they see it as a normal thing. Hence girls are encouraged to dress exposing their bodies. Premarital sex has become the norm of the society. Some Christian youths find it difficult to cope in this kind of environment' hence, they fall into this ungodly act.

➤   **Pressure:** pressure from parents, friends, peer group, lecturer, boss, future partners. Some men do mount pressure physically on their partners while some ladies mount pressure on their partners by dressing carelessly exposing their nakedness to seduce men. Some male bosses in place of work do mount pressure on their female workers; they want girls that can work for them.

➢ **Covetousness:** greed for money, wealth and position is another cause of premarital sex. Some ladies want money at all costs hence they are ready to use their bodies to get it by sleeping around with men.

➢ **Indiscipline:** lack of discipline has led many singles into the dungeon of premarital sex.

➢ **Wrong association:** this has led many students to destruction. Show me your friends and I will tell you who you are.

➢ **Ignorance:** lack of good sex education has led many youth into premarital sex some went it not knowing what they were doing.

➢ **Wrong information:** since parents have refused to educate their children on the subject and the church is not forth coming with anything meaningful, the youth have resorted to any information they can get from anywhere either wrong or right.

➢ **Bad parenting:** students that are not well brought up are likely to fall into wrong hands in campus leading to pre-marital sexual relationship.

➢ **Idleness;** an idle hand is the devil's work-shop. If you are idle, you may cuddle the devil.

➢ **Loneliness:** some claim they went into fornication due to loneliness.

➢ **Broken homes:** students from broken homes can fall into wrong hands in school due to the situation of their homes.

Consequences of Pre- Marital Sexual Relationship

The consequences of pre- marital sex among undergraduates in tertiary institutions are highly dreadful. According to Omoegun (2015), if there is one important are where the adolescents' relations to their problems can be terribly marked, it is on the dangers and consequences inherent in premarital sexual activities in tertiary institution. Once the students decide to have sex before marriage, a number of consequences which are not pleasant await him or her.

Some of the consequences of pre- marital sex are as follows:

i. **Emotional Imbalance and Depression:** Experts in both medical and education field have been very concerned about the issue of premarital sex among students in tertiary institution. The emotional side effect of premarital sex are also damaging to a young woman. One of the most common consequences of teenage sexual activity is depression. Girls who are sexually active are more than three times as likely to be depressed as girls who are abstinent. Even if a girl experiments with sex once, research shows an increased risk of depression. Also consider the fact that the rate of suicide attempts for sexually active girls (aged twelve to sixteen) is six times higher than the rate for virgins

ii. **Change in Appearance:** students who have had sex outside of marriage begin to look differently physically. They begin to look old and worn. Like toys that have been used over and over again begin to lose its physical appeal, so does a person who continually has sex outside of marriage. Many try to mask this "used up" look by adding ore make-up or wearing more revealing clothes to take the attention off face and put it on their body. Many girls who are sexually active and taking birth control gain up to 25 lbs. The unnecessary weight gain can also alter your appearance. I personally recognized a change in my physical appearance after I lost my virginity(American journal of preventive medicine, 2015

iii. **Teen pregnancy:** premarital sex among students in tertiary institutions often leads to unplanned pregnancies. Students however have more odds stacked against them then older women do. Statistics suggest teens are two times more likely to die in childbirth or pregnancy than older women are. They have difficult deliveries, scarring, stretch marks, low birth weight babies, along with the standard sagging the breast and tummy, weight gain, nausea, tear, and dark circles under their eyes.

iv. **Sexually Transmitted Disease (STD):** the spread of disease through sexual contact is often associated with premarital sex among students in tertiary institutions. STD's reveal themselves through burring, itching, oozing, and pus filled sores on your genitals. Now that's gross! Even if you don't visibly see a sore on your genitals it does not mean that you have not been infected.

v.   **Misconception about Sex:** sex in it, it is wrong at any age; but premarital sex may harm the mental development of students in several forms. Premarital sexual experiences, many a times, lead to the misconception that sex is to be enjoyed at whatever ways possible. Forced premarital lovemaking will lead to mental depression and dilemma. Another danger is possible exchange of diseases; as premarital partners may not be aware of diseases that spread through intercourse. Getting pregnant through premarital sex is another disaster. Emotional imbalances and guilt feeling could be the result of most premarital sexual affairs.

Conclusions

From the above discussion, the following conclusion could be safely made;

a)   Students in tertiary institutions in Anambra state have various permissive attitudes towards premarital sex.

b)   Many factors influence the students' attitudes in tertiary institutions in Anambra state towards premarital sex, such as showing off, satisfying sexual urges and the likes.

c)   Male and female students have almost the same rate of permissive attitude towards premarital sex but male are more permissive.

Counseling Implications

Some of the counseling implications are;

1.   Counselors are needed in tertiary institutions to teach the adolescents the need to abstain from sex until marriage.

2.   Counselors should encourage adolescents to refrain from watching pornographic materials and obscene film as these have adverse effects on their sexuality.

3.   There is need for counselors to intimate the youth on the consequences of indecent dressing, imitating or copying fashion that exposes their bodies. They are also be given tips on how to make right choices in terms of dressing.

Recommendations

It was recommend that, early sex education should be given to children, regular campaign and public awareness on sex before marriage should be carried out and that parents, government and general public need take it upon themselves to bring their own quota to the education and the reduction of sex before marriage. Posted to guide young people towards making correct and informed reproductive health decisions.

References

Adimma, J.I.B and Okeke, A.O.(2005) Contraception Awareness and Practice among Nigeria Tertiary School Girls. *West African Journal of Medicine*, 14, 34-37

American Journal of Preventive Medicine,(2015). *Sexual Behavior among Students in Tertiary Institutions;* USA

Centre for disuse control and prevention (2010) *Youth Risk Behavior Surveillance.* USA-5: 1- 42.

Hazzaz, M .D.Bin, K., Zubairu, I. and Isa, S.A.(2005). Sexual Behavior among Students in Tertiary Institutions in Kano, Northern Nigeria; *Journal of Community Health and Primary Care,* 16, 17-22.

National population commission (NPC). Nigeria and ORC Macro (2009), Nigeria Demographic and Health Survey 2009; Calverton.

Omoegun, D. (2015). Sexual Risk Behavior of Street Youths in South West Nigeria. *East African Journal of Public Health.* 6,274- 279.

Omoni, G.E and Onoyase, A. (2103) Inappropriate Sexual Behavior as Perceived by Students of Institute of Education, Delta State University, Abraka: Implications for Counseling. *Delta Journal of Guidance and Counselling, a research journal;* 1 (1), 23.

Umeonoihu, O. S. (2012). Adolescent Reproductive Health in Nigeria, the Role of the Family. *WOSSRI News*, 11, 1- 4

Umeonoihu, O.S. (2012). Adolescent Reproductive Health in Nigeria, the Role of the Family. *WOSSRI News*, 11- 1-4.